HORSE SENSE
AND
STABLE THINKING

100+ WAYS TO STAY
SAFE WITH HORSES

PAT PARELLI

CONTENTS

"HORSEMANSHIP CAN BE OBTAINED naturally through understanding and psychology vs mechanics, fear, and intimidation." I said these words at my first clinic in March of 1982. Since that time, I have dedicated my life to helping horse lovers, such as you, find as much joy and fulfillment as possible from the lives of their horses. To date I have been able to support over a million horse lovers through books, audio, videos, and live seminars. It is a privilege to coach this many people, and in doing so, I have also learned a lot about people! I have noticed the patterns many horse owners adopt when they're mad, frustrated, scared, etc.

To be safe with horses, we have to start by understanding what makes horses tick. You've probably heard horses are prey animals, and humans are predators. But it is likely that went in one ear and out the other because we know we're not going to eat them—we love them. Prey vs predator in this context isn't about hunting. It is basically how we think and relate to one another. Horses as prey animals think and feel very differently than we do.

We have a tendency to strategize and plan, which to a prey animal is pressure. A prey animal adjusts and reacts to stimulus constantly, so to be perceived as a trustworthy leader, we must learn to balance our plans and goals by adjusting to what shows up in the moment and by not being too regimented in our thought processes. When we understand why our horses do what they do, then we can create harmony.

"Have your horse understand your idea, but you have to understand your horse's idea first."

THIS BOOK IS DESIGNED to give you practical advice during different phases of your horse life. You may be buying your first horse, trailering, or even handing stallions. This book offers tips on those subjects and many more. You're going to notice several of the tips have QR codes by them; scan the code, and you'll be taken to a video that offers more explantation about the tip. All you have to do is scan the code by opening the camera app on your phone, and you'll see a website popup.

Horses are so dynamic that we can't possibly offer a "one-size" fits all approach, so the tips may have to be adjusted to fit your experience level, your horse's experience, and Horsenality type. These tips are meant to give you a perspective, a new way of thinking about the issue, rather than getting mad or upset. I do recommend seeking help from one of our Parelli Professionals when implementing the strategies in this book.

CHAPTER 1

SAFETY TIPS: WHEN BUYING A HORSE

Buying a horse can be an exciting experience, but it is important to pick your partner and not your poison. Often we trust others too quickly, and we make decisions based on emotions.

SCAN ME

#1 Watch the Owner with the Horse

MANY TIMES, PEOPLE DECIDE to sell their horses in the spring a long time after the last ride. The horse may be completely healthy and typically calm, but he may have a little cabin fever in the spring. So the first ride after a long break may be a little wilder than anyone expected – including the owner.

As the buyer, you don't want to be the person who finds out which side of the corral the horse woke up on, particularly after a long break.

When you look at a horse from a buyer's perspective, for safety's sake, watch the owner interact with the horse first: grooming, tacking up, playing on the ground, riding, and so on.

Observe, remember, and compare. Take note of everything they do, and everything they don't do.

Ultimately, this is a specific example of a larger horsemanship principle: if the horse doesn't look right, don't get on!

#2 Make Objective Decisions, Not Emotional Decisions

UNLESS YOU'RE AN EXPERT, I suggest you avoid purchasing horses at auctions because of the hectic nature that almost encourages impulsive purchases.

Make sure you have at least two weeks with which to "trial" a potential partner. Whether the horse comes with you to your facility or the horse stays with its current owner and you visit it, just give yourself time for the initial emotion to wear off. Time and patience are your friends.

#3 Show Up Early

IF YOU'VE MADE AN appointment to meet with the horse's owner, show up a little early and observe the horse and its owner as they typically interact. Does it take the owner a long time to catch the horse? Does he lunge the horse a long time before showing him to you? Does the horse react poorly to grooming?

#4 Don't Just Hop on a Pre-Saddled Horse

IF YOU SHOW UP and the horse's owner has the horse pre-saddled for you, this should raise a red flag. Make no assumptions and listen to the horse, rather than the owner.

This doesn't mean that you need to immediately get out your halter and lead rope and play the Seven Games with this horse, but at the very least you should ask the owner to play with and ride the horse first. Just determine where the horse is before you start riding.

Now, if you have the time and tools – and the owner is cooperative – go ahead and play with the horse on the ground for a little bit, to get a better idea of where his mind is.

Check the partnership aspects on the ground:

1. Can you toss the rope over the horse's back six times in each direction?
2. Play the Friendly Game all over his body, including his legs and belly.
3. Does the horse back up easily?
4. Does he offer to turn his neck around when you're standing on the ground next to his saddle?
5. Does the horse yield his hindquarters?

Ultimately, it comes down to this: prior and proper preparation prevents p-poor performance.

#5 Before Riding, Think About Stopping

IF YOU'RE TRYING TO mount the horse and he moves off, get off. Don't force it because, if he doesn't stay still when you're mounting, it's likely he won't stop exactly when you ask him when riding either.

Once you're in the saddle, test some things out: bend his neck around, rub his head, and start off at a walk. See how well he stops and relaxes. If you're confident in that, then you can take it up to a trot.

This is why I suggest observing someone else ride the horse before you get on. Then you can watch how the horse responds to cues, and whether you would even feel safe in the saddle.

SCAN ME

CHAPTER 2

SAFETY TIPS: WHEN PASTURING & CATCHING

When we enter a horse's space, such as the pasture or paddock, it is like we're entering someone's bedroom. This is their personal space, and we must be mindful of our approach.

SCAN ME

#6 Introduce Your Horse to a New Pasture

HORSES WILL FEEL ANXIOUS and won't settle in a new pasture until they have seen their surroundings and boundaries. Often when turned loose in a new pasture, they run around and around, sweating and panicking. They can sometimes even run through the fence.

Be cautious taking the horse into the new pasture. Don't just turn him loose – play some games with him before taking off the halter.

Calmly lead the horse into the new pasture and then walk him around the interior perimeter fence line so that he gets to see his new boundaries and relax into the new surroundings. This allows the horse to see where all the fences are, and who's in the pastures next to him.

Take him to the middle of the pasture and turn him loose when he is calm and settled.

#7 Turning Horses Loose into a Pasture With Other Horses

A LOT OF TIMES people will lead a horse into a pasture with a few other horses, and the horse is facing the other horses (where he wants to go) rather than the human. The moment the halter is off, the horse races away to the other horses and may very well leap or buck out of excitement, which can easily lead to the horse kicking the human.

Make sure the horse faces you when you take off the halter.

Also, if you can, lead the horse out to the other horses, and then turn him loose. This will lower the risk of the horse running off and kicking because he will already be in the vicinity of his buddies.

#8 Teach Your Horse to Catch You

HERE'S ONE OF THE most challenging scenarios we find ourselves in: we're standing at the gate with a halter and lead rope, and our horse is out there in a very large pasture. How do we get the horse to allow himself to be caught and haltered quickly?

Horses are a lot like computers: they may never do what you want, but they'll always do what you program them to do. Horses are pattern animals, and it doesn't take long to teach a horse to come running or run away when a human shows up at the gate!

Some horses see a human and they come running because they think it means "feeding time!" Some horses are ambivalent, so they barely react at all. And then other horses see a human and bolt for the opposite side of the pasture.

The first step is getting your horses to associate you with something good. That doesn't always mean food, either. It could be as simple as heading out and giving the horse a good scratch.

After that, the next step is creating a positive association with the act of haltering. It should be something you practice ahead of time so the horse has a positive attitude about haltering before you absolutely need to halter him quickly.

Don't wait for an emergency because, in those situations, you'll be tense, your horse will probably be tense, and you will want to have your foundation in place so it goes as smoothly as possible. Prior and proper preparation prevents p-poor performance, and it could save your horse's life as well.

SCAN ME

#9 Catching a Horse with Grain or Treats

CATCHING HORSES WITH TREATS is pretty common, but sometimes we run into trouble when we use this strategy to try to catch one horse in a group of many. In a group, sometimes these horses won't just come up to you; they'll come through you in an effort to get their treat.

First off, take a Carrot Stick with you, ask horses to back away a couple of times, and then invite them in.

Take some oats in a tin can with small holes in the bottom, so when you gently shake the can, a few oats come out. This way, they'll get interested without walking over you for an entire can of oats. Couple this with the Carrot Stick, and you'll be in control of the situation, which will keep you safe.

#10 Haltering Loose Horses: Halter the Easiest Horse First

THIS IS WHERE I often see people getting themselves into trouble: they want to halter their own horse first, so they get a little direct-lined, and they wind up chasing their horse around the pasture, trying to halter him. Or they end up trying to bribe the horse with treats, and then the human gets hurt when the horses start crowding them and playing dominance games for the treats.

No matter how many horses are in a group, one of them will always be the easiest to halter. After he's haltered, move him to an area out of the way, tie him up, or put him in a corral. Then proceed to the next easiest horse, and so on.

This will soon become a new logic.

#11 Don't Leave the Halter On

I CAN'T STRESS THIS enough: please don't leave the halter on your horse when he's out in the pasture.

When a horse plays, lies down, or rolls in the pasture while wearing a halter, he could get himself into some terrible wrecks:

- He could get his foot or leg caught in the halter

- He could put his head over a T-post or fence wire, pull back, and rip apart the fence and drag wire and wood around behind him or under him

The solution?

Simple: always take the halter off before pasturing your horse.

CHAPTER 3

SAFETY WHEN TYING HORSES

Tying horses is a necessity, but it has to be done with savvy. It doesn't take long for a horse to hurt themselves because they were not tied, or prepared to be tied, properly.

SCAN ME

#12 Tie Horses High and Tie Dogs Low

IF YOU TIE A horse low, he can get his feet stuck. If you tie a dog high, he can accidentally hang himself.

When we tie our horses up, tie the horse as high as you can – even above their head is okay (a branch, etc.) That way, if the horse pulls back, he has no leverage. Even horses that pull back strongly won't have the leverage if they are tied high.

Most hitching rails are about the height of a horse's shoulder, so that's not ideal. I often tie my horses to barn rafters or overhanging tree branches. If you ever visit my barn, you'll probably find at least 30 potential high tying spots in and around the barn.

#13 Teach Patience by Tying High

IT'S IN A HORSE'S DNA to escape from fear, and when they feel trapped, they become fearful. In these situations, their initial reaction is oftentimes to pull back in panic. If they learn to panic and get relief as a result by pulling back, then it becomes their new modus operandi. We need to teach our horses to yield to and from pressure in every instance when in a human environment.

Tying a horse up is a great lesson on yielding; the more he learns about yielding, the easier it'll be to communicate with him. It'll also be safer for him because the more he learns to yield, the safer he'll be if he ever finds himself in a precarious situation, like getting caught in a fence.

When it comes to tying, understand that tying a horse high teaches him patience, something many horses lack. Your horse should stand well when tied.

There is nothing worse than tying your horse to your new trailer and having them paw the shiny new hubcaps off or scratch the paint.

#14 Use the Correct Length of Rope and Two-Bite Wrapping

IF YOU USE TOO much rope when tying a horse, the horse can get himself tangled and injured. If the rope is too short, the horse can get claustrophobic and panic.

There's an appropriate length for what you want to do. In my experience, it's about 18 inches between the knot and the snap.

If you tie the horse to a hitching rail and you only wrap the rope once, the horse can slide up and down the rail.

If you wrap two or more times, it creates friction with the rail, so the horse can't slide up and down the rail.

#15 Tie to the Fence Post, Not the Rail

I CAN'T TELL YOU how many times I've seen horses tied to rails pull back and take the rail off, so they wind up running with this ten-foot board trailing behind them with nails sticking out.

They end up flying around the pasture or into the road in a panic, and if they trip, they could easily end up injuring or killing themselves, or somebody else.

This is easily prevented if you tie the rope around the post, then over the rail. Then you will have the horse tied at the right height, so if he pulls, it's against the post rather than the rail.

#16 Tie to Something Strong and High

IF YOU'RE PLANNING ON tying your horse to a panel, my suggestion is actually that you don't.

I recommend wrapping the rope around the panel and giving it a pull. If it pulls easily, go to the next rung and wrap it a couple of times there, and so on.

Continue wrapping and pulling until you get enough resistance so that the rope is secure, but not too much resistance; ensure that if the horse pulls back, he pulls the rope and gets loose, and doesn't pull the entire panel off and onto himself.

STORY

The Rodeo Snow Fence...

One of the biggest wrecks I've ever seen was at a rodeo in California. They had a "snow fence" with slats of wood between chicken wire, which made a barrier between the contestants and the spectators. Many of the competitors had their horses tied to this snow fence by the reins.

One horse bit another, which bit another, who pulled back and took the fence with him. The other horses panicked and pulled back, and the next thing we knew, about 40 horses were flying around in all directions, with pieces of this fence trailing behind them. About six or seven horses were all tied to one section of fence, running and mowing people over.

All told, it took at least 10-15 minutes to get the situation under control. Several people went to the hospital, including women and children, and many horses were injured.

#17 Three Common Knots

THERE ARE MANY WAYS to tie knots, but it's worth learning the best knots to use.

I typically use three knots when tying: the Bowline Knot, the Stockman's Bowline, and the Bank Robber's Knot.

The Bowline Knot is a three-bite hitch knot. It's the one knot that will not tighten down, no matter what the horse does.

The other two knots are almost three-bite hitch knots to the point that they essentially never tighten down.

#18 Why You Should Use a 3-Bite Knot

THE KNOT THAT MOST horse people tie is an overhand knot over the lead rope, which is fine – until the horse pulls back. Don't use this as it won't allow you to safely untie your horse in an emergency.

When you learn a three-bite knot, you know that the knot won't tighten down (because it pulls on itself).

Regardless of what type of knot you use, to be careful when you're threading the lead rope through the pattern of the knot: don't do something sloppy or jumpy and spook the horse. That's when the knot gets tightened before you're ready, and that's when fingers get lost.

The secret is to put your thumb and index finger on the outer side of the rope, where it crosses or looks like the outside of a halo. Never put your fingers on the inside of those loops, the "halo" of the knot.

#19 You're Dumb Without Your Thumbs

I WAS 19 YEARS old and had been on the rodeo circuit for about a year. My cousin and his friends wanted to go to a junior rodeo, so I decided to take them.

We loaded the horses up and drove a couple of hours down to Springville, CA. We were unloading the horses, and as I started to tie a bowline, I was running the rope through the loop when, behind me, a kid jumped up on a fence and yelled to another kid. This scared the mare I was tying, and as she pulled back, my thumb caught in the loop, and it pulled my thumb off.

It happened so quickly, and it hit me like a sledgehammer. I looked down and saw what was left of my thumb, so I ran to an EMT truck a little ways away. I said "I need you to help me. I just cut off my thumb," and when the first EMT looked at my thumb, he fainted.

Luckily for me, one of the women we'd driven down with was a nurse at the St. Agnes Hospital in Fresno, which at the time had a very good hand doctor. She took me to the little hospital in town, and they said there was nothing they could do, that they would need to amputate the rest of my thumb. She said "No!", anesthetized me, wrapped up my thumb, and took me to the hospital in Fresno instead. They were able to save quite a bit of my thumb.

About 6 months later, I was able to begin riding again, and I was visiting a friend in Santa Rosa. He looked at my thumb and said, "You got caught in a Bowline Knot, didn't you? Same thing happened to my brother! I guess you don't know the Stockman's Bowline, do you?" I didn't, and I asked what it was.

He showed me that instead of making the loop (the "squirrel going into the hole" as the saying goes) that had cut off my thumb, this knot sends the squirrel "around the hole." It's still a very effective three-bite knot, but you keep your thumbs safely out of that loop.

So, in conclusion, practice the Stockman's Bowline knot, and make sure you don't look dumb without a thumb!

#20 If You Value Your Fingers, Don't Wear Rings

OVER THE YEARS, LOTS of people have noticed that I don't wear rings when I'm working with horses. This is something I've learned from many great horsemen, along with lots of talented folks in other walks of life who work with their hands a lot. A ring can be one of the most dangerous accessories you could possibly wear when working with your horses.

When things get going fast and that ring gets caught in or on something, you're liable to lose a finger.

I've had plenty of friends who were wearing rings that got caught – particularly when handling ropes – and wound up losing a finger or two.

Rings may look nice and have lots of sentimental value, but they aren't worth losing fingers for. Outside of the barn, wear them all you want, but when it's time to play with your horses, please take the rings off.

#21 Tying While Doctoring

IF YOU EVER NEED to doctor your horse, you may find yourself debating whether or not to tie him. The answer, of course, is "It all depends." If you feel that it would be safer for both you and the horse to have him tied, that's fine – just be sure to use a three-bite knot that will come undone if he really pulls back.

Remember that when you're doctoring a horse, whether it's a new wound or rehabbing an old one, it's going to be a negative experience for him – his adrenaline will be up, and his defenses will be up.

Be sure that, when you over-focus on the wound, you're not losing focus on the rest of him – his body language, his sense of space, and so on. When humans lean down and focus on any specific area on the horse, the look on their face could cause the horse to perceive them as predatory. Of course, the human has the greatest of intentions, but the horse doesn't understand that.

If you're by yourself and your horse doesn't want to stand still, maybe don't tie him. Instead, run your rope over the hitching rail a couple of times, so he's not tied solid but there's enough resistance that he'll be slowed down a little if he starts to pull back, giving you enough time to react and control him.

#22 Approaching a Tied Horse

WHEN THINGS GO WRONG, they go wrong quickly. Be careful when approaching a tied horse; remember that horses are born skeptics, cowards, claustrophobics, and panic-aholics by nature in varying degrees. Oftentimes we humans are unaware of how we're perceived in our approach. We think about getting over to the other side of the horse or simply walking by, and just in our approach, we startle the horse.

All heck breaks loose, and afterward we say something like, "All of a sudden, for no reason at all..."

#23 What to Do If a Horse Panics When Tied

I TRY TO TIE my horse in a situation where he's not apt to get in a bind. Make sure your horse is tied short enough so he can't get his legs over the rope, and make sure he's tied high (to keep him from getting tangled) using a knot that will come undone if he really pulls.

The knot needs three bites so it doesn't bind in on itself. A lot of people think they're tying a knot that won't bind on itself, and that's true – until the horse pulls back. That's when the knot binds on itself, tightens, and won't come undone.

The Bowline Knot is one of the only true three-bite knots. Tie a Bowline Knot, a Stockman's Bowline Knot, or a Bank Robber's Knot.

When a horse panics while being tied, a pocketknife can be a horseman's handiest tool. It needs to be a sharp knife, of course, so it cuts the line quickly.

When the Stirrup Got Caught in the Horse's Jaw...

A young lady at the stables had saddled her horse up, and it was tied to the hitching rail, too high and too loose. The horse reached back and started playing with the stirrup.

Then the horse bit the stirrup and got it caught on his lower jaw. So the horse was tied to the rail and stuck, bent to the side. He panicked, flipped himself over, and was thrashing around on the ground, still tied and stuck.

I ran over and cut the tying rope. He jumped up, twirling, his mouth bleeding, with the stirrup still stuck in his mouth. We ended up cutting the stirrup leather – which was not inexpensive, of course – just to save the horse.

As you know, you can stick a horse in a rubber room and he'll still find a way to hurt himself. Well, this was not a rubber room, and it was one of the most horrific things I've ever seen. It taught me how easy it is for a horse to get himself into trouble. Had the horse not been tied with such a long line, the situation likely would have been avoided, but horses getting stuck on their own stirrups doesn't just happen when they're tied.

CHAPTER 4

SAFETY ON THE GROUND

Groundwork may seem boring to some, but you're going to spend more hours on the ground with your horse in its lifetime than you will in the saddle. Having great "ground manners" and reading your horse's behavior are crucial for a better horse life.

SCAN ME

#24 Prior and Proper Preparation

MOST HORSES ARE FORWARD-AHOLICS by nature (they're "flight" animals). Usually, something startles them, and they jump forward. So, the better the horse goes backwards and sideways, the better they do everything else.

When leading a horse, teach your horse to back away from you and sashay sideways around you. How? Win the Yo-Yo Game, and win the Sideways Game. Prior and proper preparation.

#25 Protect Your Space

MANY PEOPLE DRAG THEIR horse along, hold the lead rope close, and inadvertently teach their horse to invade their personal space. People are often taught that holding their horse close would give them more control, when in fact the opposite is true.

Give your horse a longer lead before walking. Teach your horse to back out of your space when you stop.

Walk forward with your horse on a line, stop, back up a few steps, and wiggle the rope at him. Teach him that every time you put on the brakes, he should yield and back up.

I would suggest practicing this to the point that you can get your horse at a trot, and he'll still do the exercise with attention and respect.

#26 Sideways Along a Fence

REMEMBER, MOST HORSES ARE forward-aholics, so when they get startled, they'll likely go forward, which oftentimes puts them in your space.

Start along a fence online, with the horse facing the fence.

Use the tail end of the lead rope, or the Carrot Stick, and guide him away from you sideways. Essentially, this is the Sideways Game.

This will help whenever he spooks at something, where he spooks away from it and into you. Once this game is engrained, he will understand not to invade your space.

One of the main reasons horses do this is because they're innately herd animals. When they get scared in the herd, they huddle together quickly. When it's several 1,200 lb. horses quickly huddling together and banging into each other, it's fine for them. But when it's one 1,200 lb. horse banging into one human who weighs quite a bit less than that, it becomes a problem.

So teach your horse to go sideways!

#27 Horses Don't Bite with Their Butts Or Kick with Their Teeth

UNDERSTAND YOUR HORSE'S INNATE tendencies on the ground. If they tend to bite, backing your horse will take the teeth out of your personal space. If they tend to kick, disengaging the hindquarters will take that out of the equation because the horse's hindquarters will be turned away from you.

#28 Play the Circling Game

WHEN IT COMES TO the Circling Game, be sure to have a good send before a good allow.

You need to send the horse far enough away so that it's out of kicking range.

Most horses (well-bred, overfed, and under-exercised) are feeling their oats and will just kick out of playfulness, but they're playing with a human in the same way they would with their fellow herd mates.

Have a long-enough rope (minimum 22 feet) and send the horse out and around. When it's time to bring the horse back, make sure your hindquarter disengagement is solid, so the hindquarters swing away from you instead of aiming at you.

Most people lunge their horses by stepping behind the horse to push the horse forward with the whip. Instead, do the opposite: stay in the middle and send your horse out onto the circle by backing it away first.

#29 Be Aware of Your Horse's Peripheral Vision

HORSES HAVE GREAT PERIPHERAL vision; we do not. We have binocular vision, which gives us just one view of the world. Horses have "fisheye lens" vision, which gives them a completely different view of the world. Be aware of this, and be aware of your surroundings.

Oftentimes, what happens before what happens happens is the key moment. The aware horse survives a tsunami of energy because he (or his herd mates) can beat a situation to the punch.

If something spooks your horse in the distance, make sure that energy doesn't run over you. How? Be peripherally aware.

#30 Develop Good Rope Handling Skills

I CONSIDER MYSELF ONE of the luckiest people in the world for having spent so much time with the greatest cowboys and horse-men the world has ever seen. One thing I noticed about them is that they were all very good with their equipment.

Years ago, as I was putting the Parelli Program together, I realized that many people were lacking in essential rope handling skills. It's something we can (and should) learn and practice.

Allowing horses to smoothly drift, and having hands that close slowly and open quickly, is very important. Many people are unaware that their lack of confidence disallows the horse from being able to drift, both on the ground and in the saddle.

I suggest playing with your horse on a 22-foot line, or even a 45-foot line, and allow the horse to drift by having the rope slowly and smoothly slide through your hands, and then teeter them back toward you with the same smooth motion by closing your hands slowly.

Good rope handling also means being aware of the rope around your feet. Learn to "feel" what's going on by your feet, and if you ever feel your feet getting tangled, continue moving your feet. You're more likely to untangle your feet by moving them than by standing still and trying to bend over and untangle them while also moving your horse around.

The more you practice with the rope – with or without your horse – the better off you'll be. Take your 45-foot line, practice coiling and uncoiling it, tossing it with both hands, see how quickly you can coil it, and so on. You can use many exercises to improve your ropes skills. Safety and handiness are essential components of becoming a good horseman.

Practicing with ropes will also improve your handiness with the reins; allowing the horse to smoothly drift from the saddle is just as important when you're on the ground.

#31 Leading Horses: Teach Them to Follow

WHEN I FIRST STARTED helping people with their horses on the ground, I noticed a pattern: many people held their horses up close, holding the lead rope very close to where it attaches to the halter. The more I understood how horses think, feel, act, and play – coupled with how people act and react – I started to realize that this caused many problems.

When horses become afraid, they want to move their feet; they go into a "flight-from-fear" mode. When we humans get mad, on the other hand, we stop our feet, clench our fists, and buckle down and hold everything close. That's how we end up with a nervous human holding the first 7 inches of a 7-foot lead rope, with their nervous horse running tiny circles around and over them.

A quick note on terminology: "halter broke" basically means "this horse has been taught to follow a lead."

This is the goal. You want your horse to follow a feel, and follow a suggestion.

Now, this might just be me, but when I hear someone say, "My horse is halter broke," my immediate thought is, "Oh, your horse breaks halters!" Of course, I know what they're saying, but I just find the phrase odd. Anyway, back to "what to do."

Most people, at best, teach their horses to drag behind them. There's a big difference between following a feel and dragging because, if the horse drags and braces against the halter, he's probably going to brace against the reins, your legs, your spurs, and your body language.

As I began to realize how fundamentally correct our horse-manship needs to be, I recognized that what we do on the ground is what we're going to do in the saddle. If we hold our horses short, get tight, and get grippy on the ground, we're going to be that kind of rider as well.

Think about the movie "The Karate Kid." You know, "Wax on, wax off." The sensei taught the young kid all these skills that didn't make much sense at first. That's what we're doing for our horses: when we're leading our horses, we're not just leading them. We're actually training them.

You can be with a horse on the ground in a few ways:

1. Have him completely behind you
2. Have him at your shoulder

Have him out and away from you, possibly in front (if you're using driving lines, for instance)

No matter where your horse is in relation to you, the goal is getting him in sync with you. When I develop my horses, I give them neutral responsibilities: maintain gait, maintain direction, and look where you're going. They're responsible for synchronizing with my energy and my thoughts. I'm responsible for making sure the horse goes into the gait I want, at the speed I want, in the emotional state I want, and that he yields to my particularities.

Leading a horse is all about knowing that you're the leader. Horses can do six things other than stand still: they can go forward, backward, right, left, up, and down. Being a leader means that the horse does these things when you ask him to, and stops when you ask him to. Lots of people would be very relieved if they could just get their horse to stand still on a lead line!

CHAPTER 5

SAFETY WHEN CLIPPING, GROOMING, AND SHOEING

In a vacuum, you would expect grooming to be one of the safer things you could do with a horse. But in fact, it's easy for things to go wrong when grooming, if the right (or wrong, I suppose) circumstances collide.

A lot of times, we want our horses to be clean, clipped, brushed, and buffed. We think we're doing something for the horse, but our horses think we're doing something to them.

Here are some great tips!

SCAN ME

#32 Keep Three Parts of Your Body Touching the Horse

DR. ROBERT MILLER TOLD me that he always keeps three parts of his body touching the horse at all times. His hand, elbow, and hip, for example. The idea is that, by having three places touching the horse, you've got more "sensors" that can tell you if something is about to go wrong.

Let's say you're clipping a horse or checking a wound. This is when a horse is apt to jump, get defensive, strike, or kick or bite. You want to be able to feel these things; it's about knowing what happens before what happens happens.

#33 Picking Hooves: Keep Your Toes Parallel

WHENEVER YOU'RE PICKING OUT your horse's feet, keep your toes parallel to the horse's body.

If your toes are facing your horse's body and he bumps into you, you'll be knocked backward. If the horse bumps you and your toes are parallel to him (facing either forward or backward), the horse will knock you into balance.

#34 Avoid Getting Kicked while Picking Your Horse's Feet

PEOPLE OCCASIONALLY GET INTO trouble when they're picking their horse's feet in a tight area and another horse walks by and spooks their horse. The horse squeals and kicks out, aiming at the other horse but hitting the human instead.

My advice? Simply be constantly aware of your surroundings, be spatially aware, and try to avoid putting yourself in situations where your horse is apt to act like a prey animal – particularly when it involves being very close to the horse's feet. Give yourself a lot of room.

#35 Massage Before Clipping

IF YOU WANT TO be safe around horses, help your idea to become your horse's idea. When the horse isn't properly prepared, clipping can be among the most dangerous horse-related activities you can do because of your close proximity to the horse and his innate fear of unfamiliar sounds.

Horses have long necks and heavy heads, and they can sling that head around if they're frightened and trying to evade you and/or the clipper. And if you get hit with that head, it can really hurt.

In addition, these are sensitive areas, and some horses will strike and panic if they're unprepared.

First, prepare the horse for tools like clippers. To do that, you need to make them comfortable with anything that buzzes. Go to the local store and get a cheap little $10 massage unit (preferably one that sounds like the clippers; at my barn, we use the little three-legged ones), and start at the withers and massage them every day from the withers, up the neck, down their back toward the hip, around the belly, down the legs, etc.

Do it in such a way that he starts to look forward to it and enjoy it. After a few days, he starts to recognize the pattern: "Oh, I get it. Anything that buzzes feels good."

Particularly focus on the face and neck, and around the ears. The best way to stay safe with any task is getting the horse to enjoy it.

SCAN ME

I Learned the Perils of Grooming at an Early Age...

When I was young, about 12 years old, I was clipping our next-door neighbor's horse, a little half-Arabian. He was evading the clippers, and I wasn't particularly savvy back then; he swung his head around and came down on the top of my head with his jawbone. It knocked me silly for a few minutes.

Then a few years later, at 14, I had a horse tied to a tree, in a spot I used to tie my horses plenty of times. In fact, there was a sort of ground-down spot near the tree where the horses typically stood. It had just rained, and the ground was wet and muddy and slick.

I walked up with a pair of clippers in my hand, and as I turned them on, the horse jumped, which meant I jumped back into this slippery mud. As I slipped back, the horse jumped forward and landed on my foot, dislocating my toe.

For many, many years after that, the toe was totally dis-figured because it healed crookedly. And then a few years ago, a different horse stepped on it and dislocated it back into its original spot!

#36 To Crosstie, or Not to Crosstie?

A LOT OF PEOPLE crosstie their horses while grooming. This can be okay, as long as it's not being used as some sort of solution for a horse's bad behavior. A lot of horses get claustrophobic in this situation, which makes them more apt to kicking, striking, and biting (if they want to flee but can't, they'll react in other ways).

If you're going to crosstie, make sure he enjoys what you're going to do. If you can't do it on a loose rope, don't do it with crossties. Practice clipping and grooming on a loose rope first.

Have a friend hold the rope but stand a few feet away, rather than right next to the horse. If the horse is comfortable with grooming on a loose rope, it's more likely he'll be okay with the crossties.

With crossties, the most common cause of issues is when people get a little complacent and start making assumptions ("he's tied up, he'll be fine...," etc.). Oftentimes, horses get to the tying station and recognize that whatever's about to happen – saddling, clipping, grooming – is something they don't like, so they react.

Horses are sometimes more apt to react in this way if they're led to the tying station directly from their stall, so I would suggest playing with your horse on the ground a little before doing your clipping or tacking up using crossties.

#37 If Your Horse Doesn't Like Its Legs or Stomach Being Touched, Start With a Carrot Stick

IF YOU'VE GOT A horse that doesn't seem to like being touched on the legs or stomach, don't continue trying it with your hands – that's how you're likely to get hurt.

Instead, use a Carrot Stick. Remember, the Carrot Stick acts as an extension of your arm. Use Approach & Retreat until the horse feels comfortable with the stick, and put a lot of feel in there. So many people do everything with their hands, and they get themselves in bad positions. Get your horse to where he registers the stick, as "eh, that's not so bad," and then go to the next step – get him to enjoy it.

Over the years, I've worked at racetracks. I realized that those horses really enjoyed having their legs massaged and bandaged – but who doesn't love a good leg massage?!

Ultimately, it comes down to getting your horse to enjoy the task, rather than merely tolerating it. It's a progression: the Carrot Stick, then the massager, and then eventually he will learn to enjoy when you touch his legs or stomach with your hands. It takes patience, feel, and Approach & Retreat.

Don't get direct-lined about this; you may have good intentions with cleaning his hooves, clipping and grooming, etc. But if you get so focused on the task that you disregard his feelings toward that task, his emotional and mental fitness may suffer as a result.

Confidence – Acceptance – Understanding – Result

#38 Wash and Bath Properly

START SHAMPOOING AT THE poll, put a little down their mane, and then start at the top of the tail and work it down to the end of the tail. Wash the horse from the top down, and be sure to flip the mane and really work the shampoo out so there's no residue left.

When washing the tail, use some of the suds from the tail and bring them up onto the horse's back and hips as well as down his legs, using it almost as a mop.

When it comes to washing, it's not so much about putting the shampoo on – it's about getting it off. You don't want to leave any shampoo residue in the horse's coat.

#39 Get Your Horse to Lie Down

I'M OFTEN ASKED HOW I teach my horses to lie down. The answer is simple: I wash them off with soap, tie them high to let them dry off, and then take them over to some sand. All I have to do is lean down, and they're already lying down. They want to get that sand into their coat so much!

My dad had a horse named Champ, and at 70 years old my dad trained Champ to do all sorts of things including laying him down. After every session, my dad would rinse Champ off and take him to a nice sandy spot and wait. It didn't take long before Champ decided to roll, and at the time Champ committed my dad would whistle. It didn't take long before Champ would lay down and roll straight away, and it didn't take much longer before Champ would roll when my dad would bend down and whistle no matter where they were.

Make this a pattern, and pretty soon they'll respond to you leaning down, regardless of whether you've just washed them or not.

#40 Look at the Tail to Better Understand a Horse

IF THE HORSE SWISHING his tail a lot, he's emotional. If he's swaying his tail, he's relaxed.

Many times, we don't read the horse's body language, and we just kind of head on in there. If your horse swats you in the face with his tail, it probably wasn't an accident.

The tail is its own zone: Zone 5. Take time, rub the tail, etc., until he really enjoys it. If he's simply tolerating it at first, that's indicative of a bigger issue. Oftentimes introverted horses will have a tight tail, like they want to run away on the inside.

Tom Dorrance would often have his students spend time playing with their horses' tails until they could feel each vertebra and the joints were relaxed. You'd be amazed at how many joints are in the horse's tail.

Get to the point where your horse enjoys having his tail groomed, rubbed, and manipulated.

#41 Prepare Your Horse Well for Shoeing

WHEN IT COMES TO shoeing a horse...well, things can go awry pretty quickly. Remember, prior and proper preparation prevents p*** poor performance. Many people seem to think that the shoer is responsible for the horse's behavior when shoeing, but it's really up to the horse owner to prepare the horse for being shod.

Horses are flight-from-fear animals, and having their feet handled is not something they're innately comfortable with. When it comes to shoeing, we may think we're doing it for the horse, but he thinks something is being done to him. In this case, the horse's self-preservation kicks in, and that's when things can go wrong. If this happens a couple of times, the horse soon realizes what happens before what happens happens: every six weeks or so, this guy shows up, the horse gets nervous sooner and sooner, and pretty soon he's developed a phobia of having his feet handled at all.

Undoing this takes time, but luckily for us, horses rarely forget but they often forgive.

Rather than hoping the horse will be confident with the actual shoeing experience right away, practice and prepare your horse beforehand. This way, it's neither dangerous for horse nor human – in this case, the shoer.

Overcoming your horse's innate fear of having his feet handled is like the sign inside a printing shop I went into years ago: "We offer three things: speed, quality, and price. Pick two."

I recommend the "slow and right" method, with the "cost" being time. You'll need to be patient, but in time, the results will speak for themselves. After all, slow and right beats fast and wrong.

Begin at the beginning: the Friendly Game. Use your Carrot Stick and string, and then your hands, to rub your horse's legs and ensure that he's comfortable and confident with his legs being handled.

#42 How Horses Balance with a Foot Up: Lift Your Horse's Feet

WE ALL KNOW HOW important it is to keep our horses' feet clean. It's great for our horses, both in terms of their health and manners, but it's also important for us to really understand our horses' feet and what to look for when we're cleaning them. Finally, it's good for the relationship, for the horse to know that we're there to help him and not just lead him around and ride him.

If a horse is going to pick up his right hind, it's easiest for him to lean on the left front. A horse was brought to me one time, and nobody could shoe the horse's right hind foot, let alone clean it. I had a few ideas to fix this problem, but nothing worked. Ronnie Willis was with me, and he said, "Have you noticed that the horse is putting all of his weight on his right front foot?" I hadn't because I was so focused on trying to pick up the right hind. The horse was putting his weight on the same side, which made him feel like he was going to tip over.

We put a rope around his left front foot and kept his head down. Pretty soon he balanced his weight on his left front, and we were able to pick up his right hind without any problem.

The first step in preparing a horse for shoeing is getting the horse comfortable with its feet being held. To do that, I suggest handling your horse's feet daily.

Here's a good exercise:

1. Take the snap off your 12-foot line, run the rope through the eye, and put it around your horse's ankle. Lift it up and

hold it as you stand up, and teach your horse that he can stand on three legs. Repeat this with each individual foot until your horse is comfortable with all of them.

2. Then, work on the "no-hands horse shoer's hold," which involves putting the horse's ankle and hoof between your knees while keeping your hands in the air. Practice this with all four feet.

3. Pretty soon, your horse will learn to put his weight in the right spot and get comfortable in that position, while you're supporting him with this no-hands position.

4. From there, work on teaching your horse to pick up his legs for longer periods of time – one at a time. At first hold them for a few moments, then 10-15 seconds, then 30 seconds, etc., up to 3-4 minutes, and so on. Eventually, using your 22-foot line, practice leading your horse forward and backward by the front or back leg.

#43 Hammer It Out

FROM THE HORSE'S POINT of view, the only difference between cleaning out his foot and shoeing is that the latter involves you banging on his foot for a while.

Don't shoe him until he's used to the feeling and motion.

If your horse is afraid of blackbirds, get him used to eagles. What I mean by that is this:

Whatever pressure the hammer gives a horse, you've got to be able to emulate (and probably exceed) that feeling to condition your horse to accept it. Get your horse used to the motion, the feeling, and the concussion of the experience.

Talk with your shoer to learn how hard he taps the nail during the actual process. When you're preparing your horse, increase the tapping – possibly doubling it – so that when the shoer is actually tapping on the shoe, your horse thinks it's no big deal.

CHAPTER 6

SAFETY AROUND THE BARN & THE STABLE

We often get focused on our chores, and we lose our feel. It is not about feeding as fast as we can. We must remember horses are always learning and processing our actions.

SCAN ME

#44 Look for Horse Traps

I'VE SEEN MANY BARNS and stables in my life, and it seems to me like excellent craftsman – who maybe didn't have much horse savvy – built a lot of them.

When looking at a barn, I look for "horse traps."

An easy-to-spot horse trap is anything that protrudes out into aisles, like hooks. A good rule of thumb: if it's made out of metal, it's probably going to catch something (or someone) someday, and it's not going to be pretty when it does.

Look for plastic or rubber versions of these items – tack hooks, etc. – and if you can help it, attach them where they're less likely to catch a horse or human walking by.

Now, you could put a horse in a rubber room, and he'd still find a way to hurt himself. My goal is simply to minimize the additional risks caused by barns and stables when they're outfitted for looks rather than functionality and safety. For instance, I'm excited to see that gate latches are now being designed so that horses can't open them.

I try to teach my students to have "owner's eyes" in horse facilities: look for things that could be hazardous for the horses and/or the humans, and call attention to them.

Here's my mantra for my facilities: "I want everything to be safe, functional, clean, green, and handsome." In that order. By "green," I mean, "having as much natural efficiency as possible."

#45 Be Aware of Feeding Time

HORSES ARE DESIGNED TO nibble a little all day (and night, actually), and aside from the three hours a day they sleep, they're almost constantly in some sort of motion. In their natural environment, horses have their mouths to the grass or in a body of water for just about every waking moment. They aren't really designed to eat at 6 a.m., 5 p.m., etc.

When they go a little while without eating, horses can get a little antsy. You've probably got a friend who's always got a banana and a pack of almonds with them. You may not ever see them eat a huge meal, but they've always got a little bit of food with them. Why? So they never really get hungry. Horses are the same way.

This angst builds up, and combined with the horses' natural propensity to compete and establish a pecking order in the herd (for food, breeding, etc.), feeding time can be surprisingly hazardous for the human – particularly if the horses have accepted the human as part of the herd! If you're part of the herd, you're also part of the pecking order, and you're probably not at the front.

My first piece of advice is simply developing a good awareness of the situation. Don't wander nonchalantly with a bunch of food into a pasture full of hungry horses. Remember, you're in their space now. Keep your head on a swivel; you don't want to end up in the middle of a dominance game that may or may not have been directed at you.

When you're with several horses, spread the food out if you can, with 20-30 feet separating each horse's food. But again, even if this seems simple, be constantly aware of the horses around you. Dominance games don't go away just because you think you've given each horse the same amount of food.

CHAPTER 7

SAFETY WITH BRIDLING & BITS

B its go in the most emotionally sensitive part of the horse, the mouth. You must bridle safely if you want your horse to be the perfect partner during the ride.

SCAN ME

#46 What Bit Should I Use?

THERE ARE TWO BASIC types of bits: communication devices and torture devices. The latter forces horses into submission rather than teaching him to seek bit contact. On the other hand, snaffle bits and many leverage bits are designed for communication. Snaffle bits offer a 1-to-1 ratio and allow us to gain leverage by being able to achieve lateral flexion.

When riding high-powered horses, some people believe they need to use a large bit.

Oftentimes, these bits just give the horse's hindquarters more power, which is counterintuitive when you want to gain leverage. This can cause the horse to worry, prance, or dance, possibly bucking and rearing. People who use these bits on their horse think they're gaining leverage, but all they're doing is accidentally engaging the hindquarters.

You should not need a bit for control, if you're having control issues, you can do many exercises for preparation on the ground to get your horse more emotionally prepared and available for your conversation.

If you need a leverage bit for control, you probably shouldn't be riding at the time. Leverage bits or "shank bits" help you engage in high-level, engaged conversation.

Snaffle bits are great for bending, which helps horses disengage tension in their bodies, where leverage bits straighten horses and straightness adds power. Be sure to know if you need to work on disengagement or engagement before you bridle your horse.

#47 Types of Halters

JUST ABOUT EVERYONE WHO has ever owned a horse has also owned a halter. Halters come in many types, and many people don't understand the kind of training tool a halter is.

Remember, "training" can be positive or negative. If you allow a horse to learn something you didn't want him to learn, that's still training.

The purpose of a halter is teaching the horse to understand how to yield to and from pressure. Over the years, I've figured out that wide and heavy halters oftentimes teach horses to be dull and unresponsive because they learn to lean against pressure, rather than yielding to it.

With horses, the wrong thing should be difficult or uncomfortable, and the right thing should be easy and comfortable. That's why I use rope halters: they're light when the horse is right, and strong when the horse is wrong.

I've seen people using halters with sheepskin covering just about the entire thing, to the point that the horses actually enjoy the feeling of it (it's as soft as a pillow) and begin leaning into it as opposed to yielding to it.

When it comes to halters, get something simple and effective. I recommend using a soft rope halter and avoiding leverage halters because they actually tighten as the horse leans into it, which is not as effective when it comes to pressure and yields. The secret is that horses learn most effectively when pressure comes on slowly and goes away quickly: if it's light when they're right, and strong when they're wrong.

#48 Standard and Mechanical Hackamores

MOST PEOPLE WHO OWN and ride horses are familiar with the term "hackamore," and possibly "mechanical hackamore." I'd like to define the two and help you understand these tools and what they're used for.

A hackamore is a bitless bridle that can be made of rope, leather, or rawhide, but no metal. A mechanical hackamore is a leverage unit that's made out of metal and has long levers.

A hackamore is meant for lateral flexion and lateral control (bending the horse's neck to the right and left), causing the hind legs to disengage. A mechanical hackamore, on the other hand, actually engages the hindquarters. They're both bitless bridles, but one is a leverage tool (mechanical) and the other is a non-leverage tool (standard hackamore).

The hackamore is designed for people learning to communicate with their horse to gain submission through gentle pressure from the right or left. The mechanical hackamore is designed to provide lots of pressure evenly, which engages the hindquarters and sets them wide. I've seen many horses learn how to hop and rear because the rider misused or misunderstood the purpose of a mechanical hackamore.

If you really want to be safe, I recommend not using a mechanical hackamore. Rather, use a standard hackamore and disengage the hindquarters by bending the horse to the right and left with gentle pressure.

#49 The Danger and Misuse of Tie-Downs

I'LL NEVER FORGET THE time when Mr. Troy Henry said that a tie-down was "a good excuse for bad hands and not enough knowledge."

I had plenty of friends who had tie-downs on their roping horses and trail riding horses, supposedly to keep their horses from slinging their heads around. I asked, "Well, why don't Mr. Henry's horses sling their heads around?" Well, he had hands that closed slowly and opened quickly, so he'd taught his horses not to sling their heads around.

Additionally, I've known of several horses that drowned because they had a tie-down on during a trail ride. Just a quick dip in a river can lead to disaster; all it takes is one accidental gulp of water when the horse is standing in a position where he can't get his head up, and it's all over.

Practice developing hands that close slowly and open quickly. Become a savvy horseman, and you won't need tie-downs in the first place.

STORY

Riding young horses with throat latches...

I learned the hard way just how important it is to ride young horses with throat latches. The throat latch helps the bridle stay attached when the horse jumps and generally moves around a lot. This story goes as follows:

Years ago, I was a colt starter for a man in California, and he had a beautiful show horse bridle with a snaffle bit; he told me, "Don't you ever use that bridle." I said, "Yes sir," but of course that was like putting a banana in front of a monkey and telling him not to eat it.

We were starting some thoroughbred colts, including a rather impressive (and expensive) filly. I had to get my riding done before 9 a.m., head off to college classes, and then come back in the evening to finish up.

It was about 6:00 on a crisp, frosty morning, and I thought "I'll just try that bridle with the filly, ride for about 30 minutes, and put it back – the guy's not even out of bed yet." Note that this headstall had a split ear and no throat latch.

I was sort of in a hurry, so rather than playing with her on the ground, I decided to just tack up and start riding. As soon as I got on and asked her to move, she looked like a Halloween cat, very tense with her back arched. I calmed her down, and after a few minutes, decided to take a little ride down the road.

I headed down the road. About two miles down was a ranch house, and as I was coming up on the house, some guys a few years younger than me came by to pick up their friend at this house and head to school. They were revving the engine a little, and I motioned for them to take it a little easier, which they did. When they drove past, a boy sitting in the back recognized me and gave a good-natured yell to me.

Well, that startled me and the horse, and the first thing she did was buck. I was a rodeo rider at the time, so I was obviously used to horses bucking. The only problem was, when she bowed her back, put her head down, and bucked again, that headstall flipped right over her ears and onto the ground. When I pulled the reins, the whole headstall came loose.

At this point, she was running at a full sprint away from home, with barbed wire fences on both sides, toward a highway frequented by logging trucks. I had one more driveway before the highway, so I figured I'd try to turn her into the driveway. Just as I was about to turn her, she turned the other way and ran through the barbed wire fence. Luckily the strands were on the inside of the posts, so when she hit it, it popped forward and away from us.

Now we're running across this field, back toward home. Luckily she noticed a few horses eating at a feeder in that field, so she calmed down and slowed to a stop near them. I hopped off and led her home; she came out of the whole ordeal with nothing more than a skin abrasion. But I left with a very keen understanding of how important it is to ride young horses in bridles with throat latches.

CHAPTER 8

SAFETY WITH CINCHING & SADDLING

You would assume the simple act of saddling your horse wouldn't require a whole lot of thinking, but I've seen enough seemingly unbelievable situations that I believe it's definitely worth investigating. For example, I once saw someone saddling their horse up next to a hitching rail; they threw the cinch over the horse and through the rail without realizing it, and cinched the horse onto the hitching rail!

Now, that's a pretty obvious – and comedic – example, but you can do a lot of simple things to keep cinching and saddling from turning dangerous.

SCAN ME

#50 Tighten the Cinch

YOU WANT TO AVOID two negative and potentially dangerous situations with your horse:

1. He doesn't get tense and hold his breath when you cinch him up.
2. He doesn't get surprised and react by jumping or bolting, as he may if the cinch is tightened all at once.

I recommend tightening the cinch 3-4 times before mounting.

Before you saddle your horse, play with him on the ground for a little while and give him a chance to loosen up a little, warm up his muscles, and move around. After that, gently cinch the saddle to the point where, when he moves around, the saddle doesn't come off.

After 5-10 seconds, tighten it a little more snugly.

Move him around a little bit more, and then tighten it again.

#51 How Tight Should the Cinch Be?

IF YOU CAN'T STAND in one stirrup for about 10 seconds without the saddle sliding, your cinches aren't tight enough.

When mounting, check this by holding your position in the stirrup for about 10 seconds before mounting. If your saddle begins to slide down on that side, hop down and tighten the cinches a little more.

Keep your horse's body type in mind: some horses have narrow bodies and high withers; these horses don't need to be cinched quite as much. Other horses are as round as a 50-gallon barrel; these horses often require a little more testing and tightening.

If you're roping, reining, riding up and down steep terrain, or doing other athletic activities that require a lot of movement on your horse's part, you should stop and re-cinch often because that much movement will cause the cinches to loosen over time.

Most Western saddles have a latigo on one side and a billet on the other. I recommend having latigos on both sides; I've had plenty of billets rot and break over time. If you have latigos on both sides, you'll be able to reliably cinch your saddle evenly from both sides.

#52 Saddling & Unsaddling: Always Follow This Order

WHEN UNSADDLING A HORSE, the breast collar comes off first, then the back cinch, and then the front cinch last.

When saddling a horse, the front cinch goes on first, then the back cinch, and the breast collar last.

This is a lot like putting your clothes on, you'd put your socks on then your shoes – it is hard to take your socks off without taking your shoes off first.

Having a sequence like this helps make sure the saddle doesn't get stuck on your horse with just the back cinch or just the breast collar.

STORY

My Brand New Saddle & the Hitching Rail...

When I was a young man, I had a brand new saddle with front and back cinches and a breast collar. I was unsaddling a young horse, and as I undid the cinches (with the breast collar still attached), my English pointer dog ran directly under the horse and the hitching rail. The horse jumped back and the saddle slid, but it was now attached closer to his neck. This spooked him even more, so he pulled back and broke the hitching rail. Within about five seconds, this horse – with the saddle swinging from his neck and a piece of the hitching rail trailing behind him – was about 100 feet away and still running.

I did hundreds of dollars in damage to this new saddle, the horse had to be attended to by a veterinarian (which was pretty expensive for a young man making $1.10/hour back in the 1960s), and obviously the rail needed some serious repairs. But I learned the million-dollar lesson about the order in which to saddle and unsaddle.

#53 Maintain Your Saddle and Keep It Safe

AS A PIECE OF equipment, the saddle can often be taken for granted, but a rider's life truly depends on the saddle.

Remember that saddles are made out of leather, and leather is skin. What's good for skin? Soap, water, and oil.

I've held clinics all over the world, and I've seen many saddles – or pieces of saddles – that caught my attention for a potentially disastrous flaw. I believe I've saved quite a few wrecks from happening because of this, and it ultimately comes down to two things:

1. Take care of your equipment.

2. Know what to look for.

I use olive oil on the leather pieces of my saddle, particularly underneath, which is an area that is often ignored or forgotten. Other saddle components occasionally don't receive enough maintenance, including the latigos and/or the cinches. Check your latigos at all times, particularly where they attach, near the D-rings of the saddle; the material will develop cracks and will wear thin over time, often breaking at the exact moment you really don't want it to.

Check the stirrups often, particularly on Western saddles. Where the stirrup attaches to the stirrup leathers and the fender, there's a small strap that keeps the stirrup in place.

Without this strap, the stirrup is much more likely to flop around out of place, which makes it far easier to get your foot caught. There's no more vulnerable position than having your head on the ground and your foot caught in the stirrup.

Taking a little extra time for real saddle maintenance – just a day or two every couple of months – can make all the difference between consistently safe rides and disaster.

CHAPTER 9

THE DYNAMICS OF MOUNTING & DISMOUNTING

Mounting and dismounting from a horse reminds me of flying an airplane. It isn't usually the flying part that gets people in trouble; it's the takeoffs and the landings. My insurance agent recently told me that almost all horse-related claims he receives are a result of mounting and dismounting accidents. Even when someone gets bucked off, it's technically a "dismounting," isn't it?

Here are some safety policies and procedures for mounting and dismounting, which hopefully will become modus operandi for you.

For the purposes of this section, I'll say that mounting typically occurs on the left side of the horse, so when I refer to placing your left hand or right foot in a certain position, it's implied that you're mounting from the left.

SCAN ME

#54 Make Sure He's in the Mood

MAKE SURE HE'S IN the mood to be mounted. Don't just saddle up and get on.

Play with him on the ground, and figure out where he is mentally, emotionally, and physically. Sometimes, a horse is just not in the right mindset ("woke up on the wrong side of the corral") or he is just "feeling his oats" as many say.

Taking a few moments to see how your horse feels, then going back to focus on the preparation can make a world of difference to the quality of the ride.

#55 Get Your Horse's Foot Position Right When Mounting

A HORSE WHOSE FRONT feet are narrow and back feet are wide isn't balanced and braced; he's ready to move!

Mounting is safest when the horse is standing still, in the right frame of mind, and is braced for your weight, with his front feet wide and his back feet narrow.

#56 Mounting Without Aids: Step 1 – Rock the Saddle Before Mounting

IN THIS INSTANCE, I consider "aids" to be anything that helps with the mounting or dismounting process: a mounting block, a fence, or a buddy.

Get a hold of the saddle horn or pommel and rock the saddle back and forth, particularly toward you, so the horse understands to brace himself with this movement.

The best position for the horse when being mounted is having his front feet in a wide position and his hind feet in a narrow position. If it's the opposite (narrow front feet, wide back feet) when you step into the stirrups, he will get off balance and have his hindquarters in a power position, which allows him to charge off, rear, buck, etc.

#57 Mounting Without Aids: Step 2 – Reins & Mane

A LOT OF PEOPLE put themselves in jeopardy when mounting because it seems logical to put your left hand on the horn or pommel and your right hand on the cantle. This is the most logical system...for getting yourself into trouble. This is called climbing on the horse: anyone can climb on and hold on.

Instead, get your left hand on the reins and the mane, and your right hand on the horn or pommel (assuming you're mounting from the left). This is mounting the horse, and horsemen know how to mount safely for an excellent ride.

#58 Mounting Without Aids: Step 3 – Look the Horse in the Eye

YOU WANT TO AVOID surprising your horse: don't mount him quickly without warning.

Instead, get yourself into a position where you have the best chance of staying safe, no matter what happens. To do this, you need to look your horse in the eye when mounting, not at the saddle, at your feet, or over his back.

Step halfway up, with your inside hip touching the saddle, and hesitate. Look the horse in the left eye, then lean over and look him in the right eye, asking for permission to put your leg over and sit in the saddle.

If he seems comfortable and confident, and if he gives you permission, you can continue mounting.

#59 Mounting Without Aids: Step 4 – Face Forward When Mounting

A COMMON MISTAKE I notice when people are mounting is this: they grab ahold of the saddle horn or pommel with one hand and the back of the saddle with the other hand, and they mount as if they're climbing a ladder. Their belly button is directly facing the horse, as opposed to facing forward.

Why is this unsafe? Because if the horse moves forward or backward, your momentum is going to take you sideways, and down you go. Whereas if your hips and belly button are facing forward and your horse moves, you're in a better position to handle that inertia.

#60 Mounting Without Aids: Step 5 – Get the Right Control of the Reins

FOR THE PURPOSE OF this explanation, let's say you're mounting on the left side.

If you have the right (non-mounting-side) rein under more control than the mounting-side rein, your horse may swing his hindquarters toward you, which will knock you off balance, and you'll likely wind up underneath him and his feet.

If you have equal control of both right and left reins, you could potentially pull your horse off-balance and toward you, which could result in him falling onto you.

If you don't have control of either rein, your horse could bolt, buck, rear, and so on.

When you get on a horse, make sure that you have control of the rein on that side of the horse (if you're mounting on the left, it's the left rein; right side, right rein).

If the left rein is shorter and in control when you mount on the left side, and your horse decides to move, his hindquarters are going to swing away from you. This allows you to safely step down and reassess the situation.

#61 Make Mounting Safe by Practicing a Two-Motion Mount Drill

A LOT OF PEOPLE just walk up like John Wayne and try to get into the saddle in one big swing, but this doesn't give the rider any time to assess the horse.

When you go to mount your horse, don't do it in one fluid motion. By using two separate motions, you actually make the process safer.

Here are the two motions you want to do: one from the ground to the stirrup with your right leg hanging, and then one swinging your right leg up and over the horse.

1. Here's the easiest way to practice this: when you dismount your horse, get your left hand on the reins and the mane, and your right hand on the horn or pommel (with a little bit of rein in that hand as well, for stability). Take your right foot out, let it sit for a moment, and instead of going all the way down, do this:

2. Swing your right leg over and put it next to the horse's left side (left foot still in the stirrup) and touch the ground with your right toe.

3. Look him in the eye. Ask for permission.

4. If the answer is yes, swing your leg back over the horse into its original position.

5. Then swing it back off.

6. Then back on.

7. Repeat.

If the horse is standing still, try it on the other side as well.

#62 Teach the Horse that Standing Still Is a Positive Pattern

YOU PUT YOUR LEFT hand on the horn and your right hand on the cantle, so you're looking across the horse. If the horse moves in any direction, you're in an awkward position, and you're probably going to fall, and most likely end up underneath his feet.

However, if you turn your head and look him in the eye asking permission, and turn forward slightly so your right hip is against the saddle and your right leg is dangling down by the horse's side, you are in a position where it's easy to step down again.

Don't proceed with swinging your leg over until he's standing still. Remember to push and pull the saddle horn until he's braced his feet in a standing-still position: front feet wide, back feet narrow.

It's imperative to teach horses that standing still is a positive pattern, and this two-step process encourages that.

#63 Properly Mount from the Opposite Side

DON'T ALWAYS MOUNT YOUR horse from the left side. This "rule" came from the military, and unless you're riding with a sword, it is OK to mount from the "off" side. There may be times where you can only safely mount from the right, and you want to practice this beforehand.

The best way to learn to mount from the opposite side is learning to dismount from the opposite side. Use the same procedure described above, just with the hands and feet reversed to reflect your new position.

#64 Carefully Mount Bareback

A LOT OF PEOPLE, when they mount bareback, crawl up and sit quite a way back, near the hips. At this moment, they're in an awkward position if the horse moves because they'll either tip backward or sideways off the horse, or tip forward and grab whatever they can. Basically, they look like a frog on a rocket.

When you're on top of the horse, initially sit with your seat bone up near the withers. I call this spot the "rider's groove" because the rider is in a good position to adjust in case the horse moves.

If someone is helping you mount bareback, both of you should have a hold of the rein and the mane, and both of you should understand your responsibilities.

1. The person mounting needs to put forth the effort of actually getting up and over, onto the horse's back. The person helping needs to be in the proper position:

2. Spread your legs

3. Lock your knees

Hold the soon-to-be rider's ankle

Then, when the rider is up, push with the left leg (if mounting from left) and push off against the helper's cupped hand. It's important that the helper isn't "pushing" the rider up. Not only could this hurt the helper's back but it could also give an unexpected surge upward and forward, which could send the rider over the other side of the horse!

Why is it important that both of you are holding the rein and the mane? If the helper isn't "attached" to the horse by the rein and mane, he can't do anything if the horse moves when the rider is halfway up. This is how the rider ends up falling.

SCAN ME

#65 Dismounting: Don't Be Cavalier

MANY PEOPLE ARE TOO cavalier, and their foot gets stuck in the stirrup as they dismount, and then the stirrup comes off, slaps the horse on the side and surprises him, and the rider wakes up in the hospital.

Make sure your horse knows you're about to dismount.

If dismounting on the left, grab the mane and the rein with your left hand, and the rein and the saddle horn with your right hand.

Take your right foot out of the stirrup, and hesitate. Then take your leg halfway off and step down or slide off.

#66 Teach Your Horse to Side Pass Toward You

THIS IS A SKILL I recommend everyone teach his or her horse. The first time I understood the importance of this was when I'd been kicked and couldn't really bend my left leg, so for about two months I couldn't mount without standing on something. During that span, I always mounted by having my horse side pass over to me as I stood or sat on something high. I only wish I'd taught my horses this skill before I'd gotten hurt!

Standing on a mounting block, or sitting on a fence, use a Carrot Stick to teach the horse to swing his hips away from you, both directions, and then reach over the top of his hips with the stick to get him to side pass over to you. Rub him with the stick when he does it.

This is something you want to do on principle: when you lift your stick over to his opposite hip, he should side pass toward you.

You can use the back porch or a pickup truck – anything that gives you enough leverage to effectively reach over him to give him the cue.

#67 Never Mount a Horse When He's Tied Up

ONE OF THE EASIEST ways to get hurt is to mount a horse that is tied up. The horse is a dynamic animal: he's got a mind, he's got emotions, and he's got a body. Horses perceive the world differently than we do, and their logic for survival is completely different from our logic. He could very easily perceive the situation as this: feeling unable to escape as a large predator climbs onto his back. That's when survival instinct kicks in, and things can go very wrong, very quickly.

Though this seems like common sense, I've seen more than enough wrecks over the years with this exact scenario to warrant addressing it in this book!

Simply, always untie your horse before mounting.

CHAPTER **10**

RIDING SAFELY

No matter what your dream is with horses – if you dream to work cattle, trail ride, or ride down center line – each of those dreams involves harmony. Make sure you're setting yourself up for harmony so that you will continue developing and reaching for your dreams, not your nightmare.

SCAN ME

#68 Never Ride a Horse You Haven't Seen Ridden

WHEN IT COMES TO riding, there are two kinds of horses: rideable horses and unrideable horses. And, for the sake of clarity, there are actually two kinds of unrideable horses: those who refuse to let you ride, and those who have never been ridden before and don't understand it.

Don't assume that every horse you encounter is rideable, particularly if it's a horse you've never interacted with before.

Whether you're heading out to look at an unfamiliar horse with the intention of purchasing him, or just for a casual ride, my suggestion is that you watch the owner ride the horse first. If that ride looks good to you, then you can go ahead and prepare to ride.

#69 First Ride After a Long Break

AFTER A LONG WINTER without any riding, our minds are often full of memories of the great rides we had the previous autumn, many months ago. In remembering this, of course, we sometimes forget that those great rides took place after riding all summer, building up to that. Now, your horse hasn't been ridden for months.

All of a sudden, for "no reason at all," that horse overreacts (rearing, bucking, or otherwise blowing up).

Keep track of how long it's been since your horse has been ridden, and be particularly cautious after long breaks.

#70 Keep Your Reins from Getting Too Short

PEOPLE OFTENTIMES MISTAKENLY ASSUME that keeping their horses on very short reins (or, when on the ground, short lead lines) will give them more leverage over their horses. In fact, it can have the opposite effect.

Horses have trifocal vision. When a horse wants to look in the distance, he tips his nose up in order to see. As you can imagine, when the reins are overly short and the horse feels he can't lift his head to see farther away, this can result in panicking.

Horses are born skeptics, cowards, claustrophobics, and panic-aholics by nature. This means that when they feel constrained, it brings up these characteristics, which can manifest in bucking, rearing, etc.

Riding on a loose rein helps horses become more confident because it allows them to move their heads around freely, see into the distance, and get comfortable with their surroundings. Now, please don't interpret this as "loose reins = good, contact = bad." At Parelli, we dedicate half of our entire riding program to riding with bit contact. Just be aware that super-short reins may make a tense horse more tense.

#71 Better Back-Up = Better Brakes

THE BETTER YOUR HORSE backs up, the better he'll do everything else, including stopping. Think of backing as going south, and walking/trotting/cantering as going north. If you want your horse to go south, you first need to halt his momentum heading north. Backing is what provides the brakes because stopping the forward momentum is the first step of backing.

Play the Yo-Yo Game, both on the ground and in the saddle, because it equalizes your horse's north and south on a straight line.

Practice transitions (trot/walk/stop, canter/stop/back, etc.). This will improve your horse's north and south, as well as your overall communication with him.

#72 Practice Controlled Catastrophe

THIS IS LIKE A fire drill: practicing for the unimaginable. Rather than avoiding difficult situations altogether, I suggest riders put themselves in situations where their horses feel slightly uncomfortable and practice there. Figure out your horse's thresholds.

Don't let your horse turn tail toward what scares him. Rather, relax and have him face it, and allow him to drift backward or sideways, but keep him facing the "danger."

In clinics, I often ask the riders to have their horses facing me at a standstill. I start shaking my Carrot Stick (with a plastic bag attached), lightly at first, to see if the horses try to leave. If I can get the riders to stay focused on me and keep their horses facing me, they're succeeding as partners.

It's our job to remain calm, cool, and collected. We can't get tight in our bodies because that's when we inadvertently squeeze the horse with our legs and cause him to feel claustrophobic.

With a little guidance, the horse is able to make good decisions and remain left-brained; he'll understand he can depend on you. But, of course, it takes practice. With practice, you'll be able to react quickly and correctly when the unexpected happens.

SCAN ME

#73 Complete the Trombone Drill

WHEN YOU'RE RIDING A horse and his emotions are going up, one thing you can do is bend his neck around. This does two things:

It prevents him from moving forward quickly.

It disengages the hindquarters (where the true "horsepower" is) by causing the hind legs to cross over one another during strides.

Unfortunately, what often happens is that, when a horse starts to panic, the rider in turn starts to panic, and the rider's immediate reaction is to pull on the reins.

So, to avoid that, here's a useful drill for the next time you're in the saddle.

Hold the reins in both hands, evenly at the top. Then put your hands together, transfer the top of both reins to one hand, and slide the other hand up and down the reins three times, as if you were playing a trombone. Then alternate hands and do the same.

Do this at the halt, walk, trot, and canter.

You can be creative with this exercise and improve your dexterity. For example, try alternating every hand each time (left hand down, right hand down, left hand down, right hand down, etc.).

Think of this exercise like a fire drill in school. You're practicing and preparing for that possible disaster. You're creating positive habits, to the point that in an actual emergency, it's second nature.

#74 Spurs and the Sideways Game

BELIEVE IT OR NOT, spurs may one day save your life – or your horse's life. Spurs are more effectively designed for directing your horse sideways, rather than forward or backward. The better your horse goes sideways, the better he does everything else; conversely, the worse he goes sideways, the worse he does everything else.

There's nothing more dangerous than a horse that goes sideways when you don't want him to. Imagine this scenario:

You're riding down the road, oncoming traffic in the other lane. Your horse sees something in the ditch that he perceives as dangerous, and he suddenly side passes away from the ditch and into the road. So there you are, unable to direct your horse away from the cars speeding toward you.

To get your horse going sideways better, begin by playing the Sideways Game on the ground, and then in the saddle. Don't wait until you need it! I do this with each and every one of my horses.

I'm in charge of the gas and the yields, and the horse is in charge of the brakes and the turns. Use the Porcupine Game to teach your horse to yield from pressure, and use your spurs to play the Porcupine Game from the saddle, directing your horse sideways in both directions. You should be able to get your horse to move sideways from the saddle without spur, but – when used properly – these tools can be incredibly helpful for this purpose.

#75 Opposition Reflex & Christopher Reeves

YOU MAY BE UNFAMILIAR with the term "opposition reflex," but you're likely aware of how the actor Christopher Reeves – who famously played Superman – was in a riding accident and broke his neck. These two things are, indeed, related.

Horses are born skeptics, cowards, claustrophobics, and panic-aholics. This is why, and how, they survive. When a horse suddenly loses confidence while jumping, it often stops at the moment we least expect. We're just about to go forward and up, and we end up going over the horse's head.

Horses' opposition reflex kicks in for two reasons:

1. They feel insecure/scared.

2. They learn that they can get relief by pushing against pressure (physical or mental), and then throw in something unexpected at an opportune moment.

With Christopher Reeves, it seems like he expected the horse to go over the jump, but the horse stopped and launched Mr. Reeves over the jump.

This is why it's so important to understand the mental and emotional aspects of the horse, in addition to just the physical. There's so much more going on with our horses than what we can see with the naked eye. Never make assumptions.

#76 Figure Out Which Side of the Corral Your Horse Woke Up On

HORSES SLEEP ABOUT THREE hours per day, which means they have about 21 hours every day to live what they learn and learn what they live – and they're living and learning lots of things we might not be aware of – the influence of the herd, some bad experience in the past, and so on. We can't assume that our horses are always calm, cool, and collected.

Do you know which side of the corral your horse woke up on this morning? It wouldn't be a bad idea to find out. This chapter's story "The Old Man and the Parade" illustrates why. That story has held a permanent place in my mind ever since.

At many of my early clinics, people would show up a little late, then saddle up and hop on – and inevitably the horse panicked and starting bucking, rearing, and bolting. That's why I started doing ground skills at my clinics, to really see which side of the corral these horses woke up on. I didn't want to see one more person take a flying lesson without a pilot.

STORY

The Old Man and the Parade

Years ago, on an April Saturday morning in Clovis, CA, a local man wanted to be the oldest man in the parade. For the past few years, his slightly older friend had held that title, but eventually the friend passed away, so he had his chance. Now, this man had this old horse that was only ridden once a year, for this annual parade. He went out and caught him, saddled him up, and brought him to the parade starting area. When stepped on and got ahold of that bridle, that horse felt unprepared and started to move his feet. The old man grabbed the reins, and that horse flipped over and landed upside down on him. And the man never got his chance to be the oldest man riding in the parade.

I've thought about this story a lot over the years, and it makes me sad. If he had just moved the horse around on the ground a little, he would have realized that the horse wasn't ready, and he could have given the horse the time he needed to calm down. In time, he would have gotten through the parade safely.

This story just shows that we should never just walk up to our horses and hop on. We need to determine which side of the corral our horses woke up on.

CHAPTER 11

TRAIL RIDING SAFETY

Trial riding is the ultimate picture of relaxation for many people and a great way to spend the weekend. When you're on the trail, you're often away from home and away from immediate help. Preparation for a safe ride is key.

SCAN ME

#77 Fast Horses in the Back, Slow Horses in the Front

THERE IS NOTHING WORSE than going out in a group, and soon after you leave, the group becomes split up. This is not only unsafe, but it is also not training good habits for your horse. Next time you go out in a group, try putting the slow horses in front and the faster horses in the back.

#78 Keep Your Knees Safe When Riding

WHENEVER I TAKE SOMEONE on a trail ride, I explain to them, "Push on a tree to save your knee."

It's easy to move your horse's withers over when you're riding by pushing on a solid object. Next time you're riding through reasonably tight quarters in the forest, allow your horse to walk close to a tree, and reach your hand out and push off from the tree as you walk past. You'd be surprised how smoothly your horse moves away, and it's easier than trying to pull your horse away from the tree by using your reins.

Since we're on the subject of knees: when you're riding along a fence and you're getting closer and closer – leaving your knee as the likely first thing to hit the fence – don't try to turn your horse away from the fence because that'll just bring your knee closer to it. Instead, turn his nose toward the fence. This'll put his nose in between your knee and the fence, keeping your knee safe.

#79 Safely Ride Downhill

PEOPLE OFTENTIMES GET THEMSELVES into trouble when riding down a steep hill because their horses get a little sideways. The horse and rider become unbalanced, and, well, you know the rest.

If you're going down a steep hill, don't go sideways; face your horse straight down the hill, and allow him to use both of his back legs equally to balance and control his momentum.

#80 Be Patient When Trail Riding after a Long Break

CABIN FEVER HAPPENS TO all of us, and when we get that first glimpse of beautiful spring weather, it's very easy for us to think we can just run out, catch our horse, saddle him up, hop on, and ride for hours. But I strongly urge you to exercise a little patience.

Horses get cabin fever too. Not only are they prey animals but they're also herd animals, and they tend to synchronize. You get excited and anxious, and the herd picks up on that, which means your individual horse picks up on that. Horses are very perceptive.

Make sure you play the Seven Games with your horse before saddling, particularly after a long break from riding. If your horse has a lot of pent-up energy, you don't want him releasing it all when you just want a nice, relaxing springtime ride.

Keep Principle #2 – "Make no assumptions" – in mind. Some horses can become a little feral after just a few months with no riding, while others can go five years between rides and be completely fine. Figure out which kind of horse you have before you saddle up and hop on.

#81 Watch Out for the Raincoat Straightjacket

LOTS OF PEOPLE OVER the years have gotten into a predicament involving the raincoats they're wearing on trail rides. Here's what happens:

- As they're riding, they try to put their raincoat on.

- As they let go of the rein to get their arms into the coat, the horse starts moving forward.

- As they reach to grab the reins, their arms are constricted, and the resulting jumpy movement may startle the horse even more, and he starts moving at an ever faster clip. So there they are, with a spooked horse running off underneath them, and they can't use either of their arms because they're stuck in their coat.

So, my advice? It's simple, really: either put your raincoat on before the ride begins, or if it starts to rain, dismount, put your jacket on from the safety of the ground, and then get back on and continue.

#82 Tying When on the Trail

IF YOU'RE TYING TO a tree out on the trail, tie to a strong branch that's far from the above-ground roots. Choose a branch that is above the horse's head, and wrap the rope at least twice, using one of the knots I listed earlier.

If you're tying to a hitch or a high line, be sure that the horses are tied approximately 12-16 feet apart. When tying to a high line, be sure to use the high line knot (see photo).

When you're in a group, it's important to know which two horses will be okay when tied next to each other. If you've got them tied on a high line, they will probably be able to reach each other and kick, if they're so inclined. That's why it's important to "pair up" horses that are more likely to get along.

Be ready to adjust, of course.

#83 Don't Think Twice about Getting Off

WHEN IS THE BEST time to get off your horse? The moment it crosses your mind. It's amazing how many times I've heard horror stories from folks that involve the phrase "I wish I would have gotten off…"

A lot of times, the story goes something like this: they notice their horse getting bothered, and there's a chance to get off there. They chose to stay on the horse instead, things build up and build up, and then they got into some real trouble.

Use a tool like the Horseman's Bridle that has a mecate rein so that when you get off, you're set up to do whatever your horse needs you to do on the ground. You'll have a 12-foot or 22-foot line depending on how you use it, and you're able to play with your horse online until you feel they are safe to ride again. Getting off is about being safe and effective, not about the horse "winning."

#84 Don't Get Your Foot Caught in the Stirrup

I'VE SEEN LOTS OF people get into awkward situations when mounting and dismounting their horses. Most people put their foot into the stirrup and then point their belly button toward the horse, rather than pointing it forward toward the horse's head, which is actually safer. It takes a little more coordination, but it's much safer if you need to hop down quickly.

When you get out of the stirrup (whether you're using a more Western or English dismounting technique), keep your foot far enough out as you step down, so only the ball of your foot is in it. It's an awkward and unsafe position to have your entire foot in the stirrup, above your hip, when you're standing on the ground on your other foot.

Sublime as it is when things go right, the stirrup can easily become a problem when things go wrong. Practice safe mounting and dismounting habits, and always be aware of your horse and his habits when he's saddled.

When You're Caught in the Stirrup, Roll onto Your Stomach... I've gotten my foot caught in the stirrup three separate times. Luckily, my boot came off two of the times, and the third time, the adage "When you're caught in the stirrup, roll onto your stomach" proved effective.

I had a horse fall with me, and as the horse stood up, my foot got caught in the stirrup and he started dragging me. Now, when you're caught in the stirrup and you're on your back, your toe is pointing up, and it leverages against the stirrup leather, which traps your heel.

Instinctively, I rolled to my stomach, my toe pointed down, and I escaped.

CHAPTER **12**

TRAILERING SAFETY

It is amazing that horses allow us to put them into a metal cave on wheels. Having your own horse trailer and a horse that loads calmly is a dream come true for many. Remember, horses are pattern animals, and it won't take long for a horse to stop loading well if it has a bad experience.

SCAN ME

Loading & Unloading Horses Into The Trailer, Naturally

What to avoid

You can load a horse into a trailer in two ways. There's the natural way, which relies on psychology, patience, and understanding. And then there's the way that involves mechanical devices, ropes and pulleys, large groups of yelling people, and injecting the horse with drugs. In this section, I'm going to share how to load your horses into the trailer the natural way.

What to do

If we practice trailer loading naturally, we're going to see that it looks like the Yo-Yo Game. We ask for the horse to go a little ways into the trailer (maybe just his head), then back out, then a little more in (maybe his front feet), then back out, and so on. In doing this, it prepares the horse for the process of backing out. Remember: the better your horse backs up, the better he'll do everything else.

I've seen many horses who got into the trailer, got where they needed to go, and then were unable (or unwilling) to get out of the trailer. Horses are born skeptics, cowards, claustrophobics, panic-aholics, and forward-aholics by nature in varying degrees. If your horse is already a forward-aholic, and then he panics when in the trailer...well, he probably isn't going to back out calmly, is he?

Practice the trailer loading process described above because it involves both loading and unloading. It may seem like a waste of time if your horse loads calmly in on the first go-round, but it may very well save you a ton of time, energy, and stress when unloading your horse once you've reached your destination.

Let's say you're using a long trailer and your horse is near the front. If you choose to unload him by backing him out, and he starts getting scared, don't pull on the lead rope in an effort to slow him down. It will just cause him to panic even more, lift his head, and bump it on the ceiling, and he may very well end up going backward faster than you've ever seen a horse go forward.

To prepare for this, use the same loading process: lots of back-and-forth in preparation for the later back-up situations.

#85 Be Safe by Using the Trailer Loading Mantra & the Squeeze Game

TO BE SAFE LEARN to use the Trailer Loading Mantra

1. Don't wait until you're late for the show.
2. Don't walk up to the trailer and see if he won't load.
3. If he starts trying, don't increase your energy to get him to try even harder.
4. When he does get in, don't rush up and slam the gate shut behind him.

Learn to use the squeeze game.

Lead with one hand, and guide with the other. In doing this, you can send your horse into the trailer in front of you, rather than getting into the trailer and pulling the horse into the trailer on top of you. When horses panic, they typically go forward, and the potential for danger is unlimited.

STORY

Learning the Wrong Way to Trailer, the Hard Way...

I was a young man with a colt starting business. Someone called me and asked if I would start their horse, and I said yes. They asked if I had a trailer, and I said yes. They asked if I would come and pick their colt using my trailer, and I said yes. When I got there, it was a 5-year-old horse that had hardly been handled (not wild, just rarely handled). He was big, strong, scared, and stubborn, and he did not want to load into my little two-horse trailer. I took a long, 45-foot lariat rope, threaded it into the trailer, brought it back around behind his butt and up into the trailer divider, and then brought it outside the trailer.

Little by little, I would pull the rope. It would pull on the halter while at the same time providing pressure on his butt, and he slowly started moving toward the trailer. It went fine, until he got his front feet into the trailer. That's when he panicked and pulled back. His hind legs went under the trailer, and he broke one of his hind legs. The woman watching from the fence passed out, fell off the fence, hurt herself, and had to be taken to the hospital via helicopter. That's when I realized that this way of trailering was not the right way, and that's what set me on a path toward figuring out the safe, natural way.

A couple of months after that, I noticed that a horse trainer who lived near me – one who I'd seen many times – suddenly only had a thumb remaining on his left hand. All four fingers were missing. He'd used the same rope-and-pulley system I had, and in his case, it wasn't the horse that got injured. The horse pulled, and the rope ripped all four of his fingers off his hand.

#86 Tying Your Horse in the Trailer

TRY TO AVOID TYING your horse in the trailer, unless you feel that he will try to turn around in the trailer or be dangerous to another horse.

A lot of times, folks will have someone in the trailer tying the horse up before the gate is even shut behind him. Then the horse panics, which leads to both the horse and human getting hurt.

If you have a gooseneck or slant-load trailer, and you're tying the horse in, do not tie the horse to the ring you run the rope through.

Instead, throw it over the divider, and tie it to the next ring to the side of it. Then use either the bank robber's knot or a daisy chain knot on that ring, so when you come into the trailer, you don't go straight to your horse's head to untie him. Rather, you untie him first, then you open the divider, and then you can put a feel on the rope before you get to your horse.

I've seen a lot of situations where the horse is tied to the ring in front of him, so the human walks in, opens the divider, and goes up to untie the horse, but the horse is already thinking "back up!" and that's when they get injured – the horse slams to the side, knocks the human over, etc.

SCAN ME

#87 Choose the Right Order When Trailer Loading More Than One Horse

IT IS NOT GOOD to load more than one horse without thinking through the loading order. Load your most confident horse into the trailer last.

Be aware of your horses' Horsenalities and how they match/mismatch with each other.

I typically load geldings first and the mares last. When I come across geldings with stallion-like tendencies, I put them in as far forward as I can.

For the most part, I use slant-load trailers. I put horses that have any aggressive tendencies forward so their noses are tied to the right, which makes it difficult for them to turn and reach over to the left and bite other horses.

#88 Look Out for Trailer Awnings When Unloading

IF YOUR TRAILER HAS an awning, be very aware of it as you unload your horses, particularly if the horses are saddled in the trailer.

If you think the awning may pose an issue, consider leaving the saddles off the horses until after they've unloaded.

#89 To Use a Ramp, or to Not Use a Ramp?

MANY TIMES PEOPLE THINK that having a ramp makes it easier for the horse, but if a horse is already having trouble with the trailer, having to also get used to the ramp just provides an extra element to overcome.

In the end, if you get your horses to act like our partners, they can deal with ramps or no ramps.

Ultimately, it comes down to personal preference, and the relationship you've built with your horses. If you've got your horse confident with your partnership and the trailer, you can use a ramp or not use a ramp – it won't make a difference. Just don't assume that the ramp will make things "easier" for a horse that isn't confident with the trailer already.

#90 Prevent Your Horse from Panicking in the Trailer

I CAN'T WARN PEOPLE enough about the danger and damage that can occur when a horse panics inside the trailer. Remember, to a horse, a trailer can look (and feel) like a metal cave on wheels.

When a horse panics with a human inside, the injuries can be catastrophic.

In other words, don't shut the gate and try to travel if you aren't 100% sure that the horse is mentally, emotionally, and physically prepared.

Start preparing a week or two ahead of time, practice daily, and make sure he feels completely secure in the environment.

#91 Tie Your Horse More Often Before Trailering

I'VE SEEN PEOPLE WHO don't understand the sequence of what horses need, not only inside the trailer, but also in general. For example, if you don't tie your horse up very often when he's not in the trailer, he's probably not going to react very calmly to being tied up while also standing inside a metal cave on wheels.

The solution to this problem? Well, tie your horses more often! Oftentimes my horses are tied for 4-6 hours throughout a day, being groomed, saddled, watered, and so on. It's a regular thing for them, which reduces their stress when they're tied in the trailer for long road trips.

#92 Don't Tie the Horse Up Before Shutting the Gate

REGARDLESS OF THE TYPE of trailer you're using, it's ideal when you're loading into a slant load trailer with dividers that you don't tie the horse and then head back to shut the divider.

This is a little thing that will keep you safe. Think about the alternative: if the horse is tied first and panics, he's liable to try to back up at the same time that you are, and you're pretty likely to end up under his feet in the stall.

Instead, walk in, run the horse through the loop, walk away (keeping a hold on the tail end of the rope), throw it over the divider, shut the divider, and then tie him up from the side.

If the horse is in a stock trailer and he's the last horse in, just run the rope up and over the bars or the ring, then walk backward and shut the gate. I've seen many horses get tied, pull back, and then their back feet get out of the trailer altogether and may very well wind up under the trailer.

Use the same technique in reverse when unloading: untie the horse first, and then open the gate.

Ultimately, if we prepare our horses properly before loading them into the trailer and drive long distances, everyone will be much safer. Start practicing weeks ahead of time, and make sure the horse can load, stand, travel, and unload safely and confidently.

This is why I recommend using ropes that are 12 feet long. This length allows you to move around your horse in this space easier than just leading him with a conventional 6-8 foot line.

#93 Don't Trailer with Horses' Heads Out of the Trailer

I OFTEN TIMES SEE people trailering their horses with the horses' heads sticking out the windows of the trailer. Without a doubt, this is one of the most dangerous things we can do to our horses.

In my rodeo days, I knew a guy who was hauling his four horses in a trailer. The horses had their heads out the windows as he drove over a narrow bridge. A large truck drove by in the opposite direction, and all four horses were killed.

Please, if you know someone who trailers their horses with the window guards or screens down, tell them this story. Far too many horses have lost their lives because of this very avoidable problem.

#94 Traveling: The Oft-Overlooked Piece of the Trailering Process

IF YOU TURN HORSES loose in a big trailer (like rodeo-stock), the horses will rarely ever have a problem with it. They find a sturdy, comfortable position, and stay there. What is that position? Usually facing backward, sideways, or both.

If you have a horse that already has a problem when you travel, giving him a little more breathing room would likely help. One of the best things I've seen is putting a horse in a stock trailer and turning him loose in it; treat it like a mobile stall.

Once he is able to move around in there, then you can slowly decrease the amount of free moving space.

Tie him when he's in the stock trailer. Once he's comfortable with that, introduce the dividers. Once he's comfortable with that, move to a smaller trailer, and so on.

Ultimately, the important thing is putting your horse in a position where he feels safe, balanced, and confident in the trailer.

#95 Strategically Stop While Traveling

LET'S SAY YOU'RE TRAILERING your horse, and you barely got him loaded into the trailer in the first place (which I hope is never the case, but for the sake of this chapter, let's say it is). You want to stop every 3-4 hours to let your horse stretch his legs a little, but now you're in the middle of nowhere, and you can't get him back into the trailer.

First, avoid getting yourself into this situation in the first place. Play the Seven Games around and in the trailer with your horse, and help him gain confidence with the trailer. The key point here: do this before you need to head out on the road.

Anyway, back to the hypothetical situation above. Consider leaving the horse in the trailer when you stop. Horses can't really sleep when the trailer is in motion, but when it's stopped, they can just lock their legs and go to sleep. Particularly for long trips, this isn't a bad idea. A lot of times, I'll feed and water my horses inside the trailer when we've stopped, and then give them a couple of hours to rest.

Depending on the situation, keeping the horses in the trailer can be far safer than taking them out for the sake of taking them out. For instance, if you're on pavement, I've seen many horses take a little hop out of the trailer onto pavement and end up falling and injuring themselves because of the unforgiving (and unexpected) surface.

I've also seen situations where someone decides to help unload the horses even though they don't really know how, and they wind up getting in the way or getting hurt.

CHAPTER 13

GATE & PANEL SAFETY

There's nothing better than doing some fun, purpose-driven tasks with your horse, and opening a gate is typically one of the first such activities people do with their horses. It's a great feeling when the horse really starts to understand the task and is an active participant.

Of course, some people don't recognize the potential perils of trying to open a gate from the saddle.

SCAN ME

#96 Open Gates Without Getting Caught on Them

MOST GATES HAVE LATCHES that stick out toward the rider. It's happened to me, and it's happened to people I know: when I turned to go around in front of the gate, my back cinch got caught on the latch. Of course, I didn't realize it until it was too late; the horse went forward a little, felt the resistance, and panicked, while the gate pulled itself shut onto me. So the horse was trying to escape forward into a closed gate as the latch was still caught in my cinch. It was a mess, and a potentially dangerous one at that.

Other gates have latches made from sucker rod, coming down at a diagonal angle. These latches are probably even more dangerous because they are heavy and often have a rather sharp edge.

Above all, it comes down to being aware of not only your surroundings but also where you and your horse are in relation to them. Because the back cinch is not typically in your line of sight, it can get caught on things without you immediately noticing.

When you're opening a gate, bring it toward you until it's half open. Ride clear around it, stop, and relax. Make sure everything is clear; nothing is caught anywhere, and then side pass away and close the gate. Rather than riding straight through the gate, this little procedure gives you and the horse the discipline and the awareness you need.

Bring the gate toward you, as opposed to having the horse walk straight through it, nudging it with his nose as he goes. It may be a cute little trick at first, but pretty soon it teaches him to make assumptions, and it puts you in a dangerous situation.

#97 Build Confidence at the Gate

TO GET MY YOUNG horses confident when opening gates, I typically leave a Savvy String tied to the gate door, about 18 inches from the latch. This allows me to gently swing the gate door toward me once I've got it open. If the horse gets a little spooked by it, the string gives me a little added distance so I can move the horse a little while still having control of the gate.

Not only does this build your horse's confidence by allowing him to investigate the gate without being directly next to it at all times, but it also improves your handiness, along with simply giving you a better understanding of your horse's thresholds.

#98 Electric Fences

IF YOUR FACILITY HAS an electric fence, be sure that your horses are "electric fence savvy." What does that mean?

Well, remember that some electric fences simply look like wire, and if the horse isn't familiar with this setup, he could get up a head of steam and run through it, as he would with any other standard fence wire.

Also, a horse could be grazing next to the fence and lean over to reach grass on the other side. If his chest touches the wire, he may actually jump forward and over the fence, rather than backward. This goes back to the horse's flight response; it's much easier for a horse to escape by running forward than backing or turning and then running.

Ultimately, it's up to us to teach our horses the proper response to pressure. Also, I suggest putting the horse on a 12-foot or 22-foot line and playing with them near the fence, allowing them to touch it. You know they're going to end up touching it eventually, so it should happen when you're there to guide them toward the proper response.

Once the horse is aware of the fence, he will remember it from that point on; you'll likely notice him keeping his distance from the fence!

In addition to the bare wire variety of electric fence, you may also come across standard wood or metal post fences with electric components, which are typically safer for the horse than the bare wire. But the same preparation should apply because your horse should still be aware of the fence regardless.

Play with him on the ground near the fence and teach him the feel "of" the fence, rather than running through the fence. This is how a horse becomes "electric fence savvy."

#99 Handling Electric Wire Gates

ELECTRIC WIRE GATES PRESENT their own sets of advantages and challenges. Whether you're on the ground or riding, going through an electric gate can be very dangerous if you aren't prepared and aware of your surroundings.

Many people don't realize the two ways to construct electric gates:

1. When you open the gate, it's still "hot" (electric)
2. When you open the gate, it's "cold" (not electric)

Obviously, the second option is preferable for just about everyone involved. To ensure that the gate is cold when opened, make sure that while the attachment end of the gate is hooked into the live wire, the other side of the gate is hooked up to a non-electric post. This way, when you unhook it, it's not live.

In the other case, what often happens is this: the first person through the gate takes the wire and tosses it on the ground, but the next person who happens to come through isn't aware of that, and the horse ends up stepping on it, which can lead to plenty of problems – bucking, kicking, bolting, you name it.

#100 Handle Panels Properly

IF YOU'RE LIKE ME, you love the flexibility that panels offer. But while they offer flexibility, they can also be a little cumbersome and potentially dangerous if you don't set them up and interact with them properly.

Disassembling Panels: Bottom First

I've observed many people making the same mistake when disassembling their panels. They take the top section (attaching the two panels) apart first, and then lean down to take the bottom section apart. As they're doing this, the panel can very easily tip and fall onto them because the only thing keeping it standing is a section near the very bottom. So it becomes top-heavy and unbalanced.

Always disassemble the bottom section first. And when possible, have a friend or two help you in setting up and taking down your panels.

CHAPTER **14**

SAFETY WITH STALLIONS

STALLIONS ARE AMAZING BEINGS, but you have to be savvy.

#101 Even Low-Libido Stallions Are Dangerous

THE TOPIC OF STALLIONS tends to bring out the anthropomorphic side (projecting human thoughts and emotions onto animals) of lots of people. Many people react to the act of castrating a stallion as if it were akin to castrating a family member. What most people don't understand is that it's in their DNA to play dominance games with one another, so that they can gain the right of reproduction. Procreation is an essential component of what makes horses the way they are.

The lead mare is the strongest, smartest, most dominant mare in her herd; the stallion holds the same position in a bachelor herd. This herd practices fighting each other for the right to challenge the stallion in the mare's herd. As this goes on, these horses become very keen in the art of dominance games. If you own or have owned a stallion, you're probably very familiar with what this means.

Occasionally you may come across a stallion with a low libido. This horse may be reasonably docile and won't challenge you as a stallion with a medium or high libido would. Keep in mind, however, that these low-libido stallions are the exception, not the rule.

More often than not, you will encounter stallions that see you as a fellow herd member, as a competitor, as a threat, and they will react accordingly. That's how people get hurt. In my opinion, a good stallion makes a great gelding.

STORY

The Story of Peppy Sandman...

Peppy Sandman was a quarter horse stallion that came from the King Ranch. The man who bought him as a yearling paid $100,000 back in the late 1970s, which is a lot of money these days and a heck of a lot of money back then.

The horse managed to fracture its right hind leg and needed six screws inserted into his leg. Because his owners were particularly conscious of this leg moving forward, he went through his life without ever really being disciplined or controlled in any way, for fear of hurting the leg.

He ended up becoming very vicious, to the point that he got a reputation among the locals for his ferocity. He went to some trainers not far from Clements, CA. In a breeding situation, he reached over (with a chain over his nose) and bit one of the trainer's wives on the shoulder. He held on for over a minute, dragging her and slinging her around like a rag doll before she was able to escape.

Unfortunately, these stories are not unique. My hope is that, by sharing these stories, I'm able to share with you the reality – as opposed to the romance – of owning a stallion. Not that there aren't exceptions, of course, but I suggest you avoid taking that chance. As I said above, I believe a good stallion makes a great gelding.

THE PARELLI NATURAL HORSEMANSHIP Program revolutionized the horse industry when Pat Parelli coined the term Natural Horsemanship. Natural Horsemanship teaches everyday horse lovers to use applied horse psychology, meaning we need to feel, think, act, and play more like horses. Can you imagine how successful your horse life would be if you could solve your horse challenges using a language your horse understood? Horses do not respond well to forceful tactics such as whips and bigger aids, although we often result to tools like these when we're out of solutions.

The Parelli Program is a home study program that is studied around the globe by hundreds of thousands of students using The Parelli Savvy Club and The Parelli Levels Program. If you want to learn all the ins and outs of reading and understanding horse behavior, creating a solid training foundation, or resolve challenges, then the Parelli Program can empower you to do just that.

Learn more about the Parelli Program and contact one of our Licensed Parelli Professionals by scanning the code below.

Lightning Source UK Ltd.
Milton Keynes UK
UKHW041120100322
399742UK00003B/2